# The Power And Work
# Of The
# Holy Spirit

by

Joanna P. Moore

*First Fruits Press*
*Wilmore,*
*Kentucky*
*c2018*

*The power and work of the Holy Spirit.*
By Joanna P. Moore.
First Fruits Press, © 2018

ISBN: 9781621717935 (paperback), 9781621717959 (digital),
9781621717942 (kindle)

Digital version at
http://place.asburyseminary.edu/firstfruitsheritagematerial/151

For all other uses, contact:

First Fruits Press
B.L. Fisher Library
Asbury Theological Seminary
204 N. Lexington Ave.
Wilmore, KY 40390
http://place.asburyseminary.edu/firstfruits

**Moore, Joanna P., 1832-1915.**
  The power and work of the Holy Spirit / by Joanna P. Moore. – Wilmore,
  KY : First Fruits Press, ©2018.

  pages 65 : portrait ; cm.
  Reprint. Previously published: New York : Fleming H. Revell, c1912.
  ISBN: 9781621717935 (pbk.)
  1.  Holy Spirit.  I. Title.

BT122.M6 2018                                                        204

Cover design by Jon Ramsay

asburyseminary.edu
800.2ASBURY
204 North Lexington Avenue
Wilmore, Kentucky 40390

*First Fruits*
THE ACADEMIC OPEN PRESS OF ASBURY SEMINARY

First Fruits Press
*The Academic Open Press of Asbury Theological Seminary*
204 N. Lexington Ave., Wilmore, KY 40390
859-858-2236
first.fruits@asburyseminary.edu
asbury.to/firstfruits

JOANNA P. MOORE.

# The Power and Work

OF THE

# HOLY SPIRIT

BY

## JOANNA P. MOORE

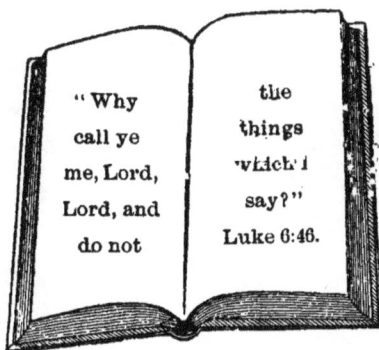

"Why call ye me, Lord, Lord, and do not the things which I say?" Luke 6:46.

"The Holy Spirit reveals Christ to the believer and glorifies Christ."—John 16:13-15.

"Grieve not the Holy Spirit."—Eph. 4:30.

---

PUBLISHED BY

## FLEMING H. REVELL COMPANY

New York, 158 Fifth Ave.   ::   Chicago, 125 No. Wabash Ave.

: PRICE 25 CENTS PER COPY.  SIX COPIES FOR $1.00 POSTPAID.  : :

# Introduction.

The greater part of the contents of this little book appeared in our paper, HOPE. We now give them in book form because so many persons have written asking questions about the Holy Spirit. They want to learn more of what God tells us about the ''Baptism of the Holy Spirit,'' Acts 1.5, of being ''filled with the Spirit,'' Acts 2:4, of ''how to receive the gift of the Holy Spirit,'' Acts 2:38. There seems to be a longing, a hunger, in many hearts for a better understanding of the work of the Holy Spirit as regards our conversion and our sanctification and how to receive the power of the Holy Spirit for the work of Christ or for ''witnessing,'' as spoken of in Acts 1:8. I rejoice in the fact that our Bible study has led to these thoughtful questions. It is a proof that the Holy Spirit is working in the hearts of our Bible Band readers. They want to know God. Jer. 9:23, 24.

This is the greatest of all knowledge. The Bible and the Holy Spirit impart to the humble and teachable believer this knowledge. Oh, Lord, give especially to me wisdom to answer these inquirers after Truth. Give to us all an humble and meek spirit while we sit at Thy feet to learn of Thee!

## A Prayerful Request.

We request that those who are helped by these lessons may make a great effort to teach them to their neighbors. "Have you found the heavenly light? Pass it on." Your light will shine brighter after you have used it to show some one over a dangerous pathway. Yes, the more you use your light the more you will have. It is like love. The more you *give* the more you have left. Do not be selfish. Take time to teach others what you know. This is one way of improving the talents God has given you. Matt. 25: 14-30. If you do not help others with what you know, you will be like the servant in verses 24-25. Verse 30 tells his reward. Do you want to be like him?

May God take this little book that I send with love and prayer to my Fireside pupils, this New Year of 1898 and make it to them a great blessing for Jesus' sake, Amen.

Nashville, Tenn., 1898.

## Preface to Second Edition.

The first edition contained five thousand, which have been largely read and greatly blessed.

## The Fireside School.

The Power and Work of the Holy Spirit is one of the books used in the Fireside School.

What is meant by a Fireside School?

A Fireside School is a school at home to which parents and children both belong. You *join* the school by reading our Bible lessons in HOPE *daily with your family*—other books follow). This is not a woman's school. It includes the whole household, especially the father, who is the head of the house.

What is the object of this school?

The object of the Fireside School is:

First, to secure the daily prayerful study of the Bible in all homes.

Second, to seek to extend this blessing to their neighbors' home.

## Parents' Pledge.

"1. I promise that by the help of God, I will pray with and for my children, and daily teach them the Bible and expect their early conversion.

2. I will be a good pattern for my children in my daily life, especially in temper, conversation and dress.

3. I will recognize the fact that God expects me to care for and train my children for him in soul and mind as well as body.''

When did this school begin its work?

It began in the heart of the author more than fifty years ago, when she saw the great influence of the home life in forming character for good or ill.

HOPE, the organ of the school is 27 years old, with a circulation of about seventeen thousand. It is a family magazine, inter-denominational. Its object is to make home the best and happiest place in the world. This it accomplishes by the daily prayerful study of God's Word, accompanied by the power of the Holy Spirit. If taken in clubs of ten or more to one address, 25 cents a year. Single copy 50 cents a year.

Those desiring to know more about the School may write to the author at 2969 Vernon avenue, Chicago, Illinois, or to Fireside School, 513 Mulberry street, Nashville, Tenn.

Chicago, Ill., July, 1912.

## Why Do We Not Give the Scripture Texts in Our Books and Papers ?

We answer because we greatly desire that every reader may use his Bible as he reads and finds there the text referred to. I noticed that the Sunday school quarterlies gave the texts and the pupils relied upon these verses in the quarterly and left their Bibles at home, and, in fact, did not feel the need of a Bible at school nor at home. The writers of these Sunday school lessons did not expect such a result, but it certainly is a fact that the Sunday school helps have taken the place of the Bible in many of our schools. If our Sunday school writers had given *only* the explanation of the text, then the pupils in order to understand that, would have been compelled to get their Bibles. Wherever Bible bands have been established they *have created a cry for Bibles, because in our lessons we have only given chapter and verse.* We are delighted to see how these lessons have taught them to love the Bible, even the little children are able to find the lessons in the Bible. We are making a great effort to get every child in the family to own a Bible even before it can read. Indeed, many of our children *now* find a Bible ready for them when them come to this world. This is a part of our Fireside School plan. Thus God's word is being magnified and glorified in the homes of our Fireside pupils.

We hope that every one who reads our little book owns a Bible. If not you must get one before you read this book; in fact, you can't read it without a Bible. Please do stop as you read and hunt up *every* text referred to. If you do not, the book will do you no good, because you cannot see that *what we say agrees with the Bible.* Oh, do use your Bible as you read this book.

### Poor, but with Thousands in the Bank.

A miser died for want of care in a wretched hovel. It was found after his death that he had twenty thousand dollars in banks, but was too stingy to use it. "How foolish! Was the man crazy?" you ask. No, he was an intelligent man, only he was a miser. This incident led me to think along another line. Christ Jesus bought with his own blood, salvation for all the human family. I Tim. 2:4. He calls the sinner to him and promises that "whosoever cometh to him he will in no wise cast out." John 6:33-37. You see how rich is the provision for salvation. Yet thousands of sinners die every year and go to hell simply because they will not *accept* of the love and pardon offered them in the Gospel. Oh, how foolish, you say; are they crazy? No, no; they are intelligent human beings, with God's Bible in their hands. There is another class of persons who have accepted of pardon. They believe their names are written in the Book of Life, and yet they go with their heads hung down half the time, saying, "I am so weak and sinful I can't speak to a sinner, I can't pray, nor do the good I desire. I can't help sinning every day. It is sometimes up and sometimes down, and sometimes level with the ground," and yet they know Christ offers a *perfect* salvation *from sin,* every day and hour. Why not accept "That ye may be blameless and harmless, the sons of God, without rebuke, in the midst of a crooked and perverse nation, among whom ye shine as lights in the world. Phil. 2:15. Why not rejoice in the Lord always? Why not let Christ lead them a victorious life? 2 Cor. 2:14. Why do they let the devil conquer them every day when Christ came to destroy the works of the devil and make them *free indeed?* Oh, you say how foolish that they do not let God save them from the devil. "Are they crazy?" you ask. Oh, no; they are members of the church and have read over and over again that God is able and willing to keep them from falling, Jude 24, but they seem to love this "up and down" Christian life, servants of God half the day, servants of the devil the other half. What if death called for them during the half day they were serving the devil, where would they go, to heaven or hell? Answer.

Oh, beloved, God has untold riches stored away in Christ Jesus for all his children, heights and depths of love and power, of joy and peace, of hope and courage for all who will *accept* of it. We may abound in *every* good work. 2 Cor. 9:8. We may walk worthy of the Lord. Col. 1:10. But we must let the Holy Spirit take full possession of us. Let Him fill us with his wondrous love and power. Why die in the midst of plenty? We have great possessions treasured in Christ. Oh, the riches of God's grace! Let us receive, and shine in the beauty of holiness every day and every hour. There is no "up and down" on the *road* to glory. The *down* comes when we get *off* the road. The road itself is *up* all the way from earth to heaven. Those who say "the *way* is *sometimes* up and *sometimes* down" acknowledge that they are led captive by the devil every day, and they say they can't help it. Such persons are more to be pitied than the man who died for want of care with thousands in the bank.

Every one does not know what a wonderful, all-powerful Saviour we have or they would *let Jesus* conquer Satan *every* time, and sing a song of victory from morning till night. Col. 2:1-10.

## What a Wonderful Saviour!

"CHRIST has for sin atonement made.
  We are redeemed! the price is paid!
He cleansed my heart from all its sin,
  And now He reigns and rules therein.
What a wonderful Saviour is Jesus, my Jesus!
What a wonderful Saviour is Jesus, my Lord!"
  I praise Him for the cleansing blood.
    What a wonderful Saviour!
  That reconciled my soul to God;
    What a wonderful Saviour!

He walks beside me in the way,
    What a wonderful Saviour!
And keeps me faithful day by day:
    What a wonderful Saviour!

He gives me overcoming power,
    What a wonderful Saviour!
And triumph in each trying hour;
    What a wonderful Saviour!

To Him I've given all my heart,
    What a wonderful Saviour!
The world shall never share a part;
    What a wonderful Saviour!

               —*Gospel Hymns.*

## What Do You Mean by Sanctification, Holiness, Etc.

You have asked a very important question. A question which should be answered by God's word and for God's glory. It matters little what *you* or *I* mean by these scripture terms, Sanctification, etc. But *what does God mean; what does God Say?* May we each search the Scripture for the answer.

The holier, higher life, "the life more abundant," John 10:10, that all God's redeemed children should live is called by different names: Sanctification, Rest of Faith, Baptism of the Holy Spirit, Holiness, Christ Life, etc. They all mean about the same thing.

## A Witness for Christ.

As a witness to what the Holy Spirit and the Bible has taught me, I humbly answer that it means to *me,* and to many others, that "Christ is able to keep that which I have committed unto Him," 2 Tim. 1:12. We give ourselves to Jesus and He *keeps* us from the

devil and from sin. Glory to His name! He is able
to keep us from *falling*. Jude 24. Therefore, we do
not expect to be "sometimes up and sometimes down,"
since we need not fall. Indeed, we have the promise "that we shall not fall," 2 Peter 1:10, on condition that we obey God's commands, and we believe
that Jesus has come to live his *life in us*, thus giving us power to obey. Jesus' power in us causeth us
*always* to triumph *in Christ*. 2 Cor. 2:14. Notice
"always." But it is *all in Christ*. We believe that
"without Jesus we can do nothing." John 15:5. We
believe that "God is able to make all grace abound,"
so that we are always ready for every good work.
2 Cor. 9:8; 1 Cor. 15:58. We believe that the Holy
Spirit is in us a "well of living water," John 4:14,
which keeps us fresh and joyous three hundred and
sixty-five days in a year if we will obey. Jesus gives
us *his* power, his faith, with which to obey. Christ
came to "destroy the works of the devil." Therefore, he is always able to succor us who are tempted
by Satan. Heb. 2:14-18.

There is another great truth that we believe,
namely, *that we keep on growing in grace after we
are sanctified,* or set apart, for the service of God,
which is what sanctification means. Paul "thanked
God for the brethren whose faith grew exceedingly."
2 Thess. 1:3. We believe our faith will have a better chance to grow if we keep on believing rather
than if we stop to doubt God and thus fall into sin.
If we keep on loving our love will "abound," but
if we stop to hate our love will grow cold. Yes, we
believe "in growing in grace and in the knowledge

of God." 2 Peter 3:18. By so doing, we "are kept from being led away by the error of the wicked," or, in other words, kept from sinning. 2 Peter 3:17. The way to grow in any virtue is to keep on practicing it rather than to stop and practice the opposite vice a part of the day as our opponents tell us we *must* do. Yes, we believe that every day we grow stronger in the Lord and in the power of his might. Sin weakens, therefore we sin not, because "*we are kept* by the power of God unto salvation" (not unto sin). 1 Peter 1:5.

## What We Do Not Believe.

We do not believe that we cannot be tempted nor that we cannot yield to the temptation. We may yield, therefore, we are constantly taught to "watch and pray." The Holy Spirit in us makes us "remember" and keeps us in touch with Christ. John 14:26. We do not believe that temptation is sin, because Christ was tempted in all points like as we, but without sin. Heb. 4:15-16.

The above is the faith of those who, like Paul, can say, "I am crucified with Christ, nevertheless I live, yet not I, but *Christ liveth in me,* and the life which I now live in the flesh I live by the faith of the Son of God, who loved me and gave himself for me." Gal. 2:20. In living this life of freedom from sin we believe that we honor Christ more than if every day we were led captive by the devil.

## What Another Class of Persons Teach.

There is another class of teachers who do not entirely deny the above doctrine. They say that God is *able* to save us from the world, the flesh and the devil, but they take the faith and courage all out of us by saying God has placed us in such a condition that we *cannot* obey, that this sinful world and our natural tendencies to evil are so strong that they cause us to *sin every day.* Their faith places us in a sad, lost, helpless condition. It is true these teachers will allow us to conquer the devil a part of the time but they *will not let us be good all day.*

God is not a hard master; with every command is given the power to obey. These teachers "limit the Holy one of Israel," Ps. 78:40-41, and turn us back into the wilderness just as we are ready to enter into the promised land; yes, and "they be ready to stone" the Calebs and Joshuas that insist on saying, "We be well able to overcome." Num. 13:30. "For the Lord is with us." Num. 14:9.

Beloved friends, "We walk by faith." "All things are possible to him that believeth." "I can do all things through Christ, which strengthens me." Phil. 4:13. Let us do as our motto says: "Looking unto Jesus." Keep our eyes on the Captain of our salvation, and not at our own sinful nature, which was "crucified with Christ," Rom. 6:6, nor at the cowardly soldiers who will insist on being conquered every day, and so shall *we* be "brought off more than conquerers through him that loved us." Glory be to God! Rom. 8:37.

## Not I, but Christ.

"Not I, but Christ, be honored, loved, exalted,
 Not I, but Christ, be seen, be known, be heard,
Not I, but Christ, in every look and action,
 Not I, but Christ, in every thought and word.

O to be saved from myself, dear Lord,
 O to be lost in Thee;
O that it might be no more I, but Christ, that lives in me."
"Not I, but Christ, my every need supplying,
 Not I, but Christ, my strength and health to be:
Christ, only Christ, for body, soul and spirit,
 Christ, only Christ, live then Thy life in me.

"Not I, but Christ, in lowly, silent labor,
 Not I, but Christ, in humble, earnest toil,
Christ, only Christ, no show, no ostentation,
 Christ, none but Christ, the gatherer of the spoil.

"Christ, only Christ, ere long will fill my vision,
 Glory excelling soon, full soon I'll see—
Christ, only Christ, my every wish fulfilling—
 Christ, only Christ, my all in all to be."

—*Selected.*

## Words of Warning.

Before we close we have one word of warning for those who believe in full salvation. Let the Holy Spirit keep you sweet and patient toward those who oppose. Remember the fruit of the Spirit? Gal. 5:23-24. Keep under the fountain, and let God fill you with *his* love and long suffering, which never give out. We are not judges, we are fellow servants. Get your Bible and read 1 Peter 3:13-17. I give the text here for those who may not have a Bible near.

13. "And who is he that will harm you, if ye be followers of that which is good?

14. "But and if ye suffer for righteousness' sake, happy are ye: and be not afraid of their terror, neither be troubled.

15. "But sanctify the Lord God in your hearts and be ready always to give an answer to every man that asketh you a reason of the hope that is in you with meekness and fear.

16. "Having a good conscience: that whereas they speak evil of you as of evil doers, they may be ashamed that falsely accuse your good conversation in Christ.

17. "For it is better, if the will of God be so, that ye suffer for well doing than for evil doing."

## Take Notice.

Notice, you are to live a pure and holy life. You are commanded to study your Bible, so that "you can give an answer to the man that asks a reason for your hope," but be sure to do it with meekness and fear. (Fear means reverence or respect.) Give your reason in a respectful, humble, kindly manner. "God resisteth the proud but giveth grace to the humble." It is only by the abundant grace of God that we are able to live this life of faith. O Jesus, help us to learn of thee, for thou art meek and lowly in heart! Matt. 11:29.

## Love's Echo.

The gospel plan of love is to "love as Christ loved us." John 13:34. "Love our enemies." Matt. 5:34. "Love those who are unthankful and ungrateful." Luke 6:32-36.

True faith produces love to God and man,
Say, Echo, is not this the gospel's plan?
    Echo—The gospel's plan.

Must I, then, faith in Jesus constant show,
By doing good to all, both friend and foe?
    Echo—Both friend and foe.

But if a brother hates and treats me ill,
Must I return him good and love him still?
    Echo—Love him still.

If he my failings watches to reveal,
Must I his faults as carefully conceal?
        Echo—As carefully conceal.

If he the worst construct on all my words,
Must I the best construct his case affords?
        Echo—The best construct his case affords.

But if my name and character he tears,
And cruel malice, too, too plain appears?
And when I sorrow and affliction know,
He loves to add unto my cup of woe?
In this uncommon, this peculiar case,
Sweet Echo, say, must I still love and bless?
        Echo—Still love and bless.

Whatever usage ill I may receive,
Must I yet patient be, and still forgive?
    ECHO—Patient be, and still forgive.

Why, Echo, how is this? Thou 'rt sure a dove!
Thy talk will leave me nothing else but love.
    ECHO—Nothing else but love.

Amen, with all my heart; then be it so;
And now to practice I 'll directly go.
    ECHO—Directly go.''

                        *—Selected.*

## Bible Lessons on the Power and Work of the Holy Spirit.

There is a Holy Spirit just as surely as there is a God, and as true as that Jesus the Son of God came to live on earth and die for sinners. The Holy Spirit is sometimes spoken of in the four gospels, but when we come to the Acts of the Apostles he is the central figure and takes the place that Jesus had in the gospels, the place of teacher and guide. Now Jesus does his work through believers who are filled with the Spirit. In Acts 2:4, we are told the Spirit gave them utterance or told them the words to speak; just the same as if you told me words to write to a friend and I would put them on paper and send them away. The letter would be yours and the words yours. I was only the agent or medium through which your words reached your friend. Every Christian worker, as well as those people in Acts 2, receives his power for service from God, and to God should be all the glory, for "without me ye can do nothing." John 15:5.

The Holy Spirit reveals Christ to the Christians. John 16:14. Jesus is still alive and at work in the world, but not as. *one* individual, but through every believer who is dead to self and instead has accepted the life and power of Christ. In 1 Cor. 3:5-7, Col. 3:3, we are told, "Ye are dead and your life is hid with Christ in God," also Gal. 2:20, "I live, yet not I, but Christ liveth in me," etc. Christ lives his life in the believer through the Holy Spirit. 1 John 4:13. It is through the Spirit that we know we have Christ living his life in us. 1 John 3:23-24. Now we have learned one office of the Holy Spirit, namely: "That Christ lives in us through *his* Spirit" which is the Holy Spirit. We have the *same* Spirit that Christ had on earth and in heaven, therefore we can do *his* work. In one sense, when we have the Holy Spirit we have God the Father, and God the Son also. Read again John 16:13-15. Fifteen tells us all the Father has belongs to the Son but the Holy Spirit shows or reveals to us all we need from this treasure-house.

The next question we ask is, How can I receive this "gift of the Holy Spirit," how can I be filled with the Spirit? We receive or accept the gift just as we accepted the gift of conversion or forgiveness of sins, namely, by faith. We have read that we are the temple of the Holy Ghost; now believe this fact. We are filled when we give up to God and *let him empty us of self.* We will be filled when we are hungry. Matt. 5:6. We will never receive the Spirit in its fullness till we feel or realize our weakness. When we see that we can't conquer Satan in our own strength, then we long for God's strength, God's power to overcome sin, power to do efficient work for God, power to rejoice under persecution as we are commanded. Then, give up, let go of the world, surrender to God and he fills us with his Spirit. You are God's property, let him take possession of you. Hand him the keys to every room in your heart. Consecrate all you have in this world to God and believe he accepts it. Now you have done your part. Keep on trusting and obey as far as you know God's commands and also *confess* that you are seeking this gift, and that you are trusting God for the Spirit's power and you have Him, because the Spirit is a gift which you accept *by faith* the same as you did forgiveness of sins.

Many tell us that they received this Gift when they were converted. Without arguing with such persons, we will simply ask, if they have in possession the *power* this gift brings. Acts 1:8 says we shall receive *power,* the power of the Holy Ghost coming upon us and then we shall be "witnesses," that is, we will testify for Him, represent Him, stand up for Him, live for Him. The disciples before the day of Pentecost were weak and fearful; "all forsook Him and fled," Matt. 26:56, but after the Baptism of the Spirit they stood up as bold witnesses, saying: "Ye have taken Jesus and with wicked hearts have crucified and slain Jesus," Acts 2:23. The Spirit gave them courage to own Christ in the midst of His enemies. Have you this courage?

The Holy Spirit gives power to be strong and of good courage. When danger and suffering threatened the Apostles in Acts 4:17-31, they prayed that they might have boldness or courage to speak God's word (verses 30, 31). In verse 31 they were filled with the Spirit and did speak the word with boldness. All the way through the book of Acts these Holy Ghost men were fearless and faithful in preaching the word, not caring for the persecutions that awaited them. Acts 5:29. The cowardly Christians who are afraid to speak a word for God are not filled with the Spirit. The pastor who fears to rebuke the rich and influential members of the church lest his salary suffer, lacks this courage. The Spirit gives us power to obey God, even though death be the result. Acts 21:13.

In John 16:8 we are told that the Spirit reproves or convinces of sin. It is not your preaching or talking that makes a sinner cry out for mercy, it is the power of the Holy Spirit following your words. Therefore there is no use in ministers screaming so loud in the pulpit, nor trying to be eloquent. These things will not convict the sinner. When the Spirit gave Peter utterance, Acts 2:4, three thousand were convicted and converted in one day, Acts 2:41. You should not try to preach nor do any work for Christ till you are filled with the Spirit which gives power to your words and work.

Paul also preached with this power. 1 Cor. 2:4-5. Have you this humble dependence on the Spirit's power for your work? The poorest member in the church has a work to do as well as the pastor. Do we all depend on the Spirit's power? If so, we will go hopefully, courageously on with our work.

Sin grieves the Holy Spirit and separates from God. Isa. 59:1-2 tells us God is able to save, but our sins have separated us from the power that can save. There is no excuse for sin. Jesus said in Matt. 28:18 that he had "all power," and verse 20 tells us Jesus is with us always. It is true Satan is always around, but the Spirit gives us power to obey Jesus instead of the devil because "we are the servant of the one we obey." Rom. 6:16. There is no use in trying to dodge the issue. You forsake Christ and follow Satan every time you sin. Dear reader, why not through the Spirit trust Jesus, who has "all power" and "be saved *from* sin?" Saved from morning to night? Matt. 1:21 proves Jesus came to *save from* sin, then why live any longer *in* sin?

Acts 1:8 says we receive power after that the Holy Spirit takes posession of us. I want you to read the overflowing verse, 2 Cor. 9:8. God is able. We are not able, but we have God's power to save from Satan, and supply all we need. Beloved, do let us stand on the promises of God and resist the devil and draw nigh to God. James 4:7-8. Some persons make a mock of those who profess to be "free from sin," but God commands it. Yea, more; he says in Rom. 6:22 that "*Now* we are free from sin." We know God is able to do exceeding, abundantly above all we can ask or think, if we will trust him. Eph. 3:20. Have you the faith that conquers sin, all the day long? If so, you are filled with the Spirit, for He alone gives this power.

It is best not to argue about these subjects but rather teach God's word. It does not matter what *I* think nor what *you* think, but the great question is, what does *God think?* God's *thought* is in the Bible, therefore let us search the Scriptures.

## My Experience.

I have an experience that came to me after my conversion which I recognized as "the baptism of the Spirit" promised in Acts 1:8. It gave me a closer walk with God. It gave me a peace and rest in God that I never knew before. This power that I received keeps me in touch with Christ. Call it by what name you choose only get the experience and live this life of faith. Do as the Bereans did in Acts 17:11, "Search the Scriptures daily" in a teachable spirit and you will see that "these things are so." Praise the Lord!

Even though we have received the gift we must keep in touch with God so that we may *always* be full to overflowing. In John 4:14 the Spirit is compared to a well of living water, an artesian well, one that flows all the time. It needs no pumping. John 7:37-39 tells us the Holy Spirit gives us rivers of living water. Plenty, only do not let the pipes that connect us with God be filled with sin for that will stop the flow and leave us barren and thirsty. There is no end to the power, the love, the joy, the peace, the longsuffering that come from being under the fountain where God can pour into our souls his Spirit. He does not give us a supply that will last for even one hour. We could not take care of it. He gives it to

us just as he does the air we breathe, minute by minute.   This keeps us always looking unto God and
trusting in him.  He is the well.  He is the river.  We do
not look at others, nor at self, but we keep our eyes on
Jesus so as to get his orders and obey promptly.  The
Holy Spirit gives the power to obey.  This "water of
life" keeps us fresh and ready for service.  Glory be
to God!  Rev. 22:17.

## Trust and Obey.

"When we walk with the Lord
   In the light of His Word,
      What a glory He sheds on our way;
   While we do His good will,
   He abides with us still,
      And with all who will trust and obey."

CHORUS.

Trust and obey,
   For there's no other way
To be happy in Jesus,
   But to trust and obey.

Not a burden we bear,
Not a sorrow we share,
   But our toil He doth richly repay;
Not a grief nor a loss,
Not a frown nor a cross,
   But is blest if we trust and obey.

But we never can prove
The delights of His love,
   Until all on the altar we lay;
For the favor He shows,
And the joy He bestows,
   Are for them who will trust and obey.

Then in fellowship sweet
We will sit at His feet,
   Or we'll walk by His side in the way;
What He says we will do,
Where He sends we will go,
   Never fear, only trust and obey.''

—*Selected.*

The Holy Spirit teaches us the things of God. 1 Cor. 2:9-16. We cannot make the unconverted understand the joy and love and peace that God has given us, because they are taught us by the Spirit of God (verse 10). Sinners do not have this spirit. In verses 11 and 12 God reasons thus. A bird, for example, could not be made to understand man's thoughts because they belong to man and not to birds; therefore a man in his natural condition cannot understand God, but God puts into our very being his Spirit, his own Holy Spirit, and through that Spirit we can understand God. Then also what we teach others is through the power of the indwelling Spirit of God. Verse 16 says we have the mind of Christ because we have his Spirit. The Spirit that dwells in Christ is the same Spirit that lives in the Christian's heart, therefore a child of God understands his Father, God, and his elder brother, Jesus; without this Spirit we cannot understand God's word, the Bible. The Spirit is our teacher. John 14:26.

The Holy Spirit is our comforter. This is the dearest name for the Holy Spirit, the Comforter. John 14:16-26; John 15:26; John 16:7, gives us this name for the Spirit. Jesus was now to leave them, and when the Holy Spirit came to them he brought with him Jesus, and of course that was a glorious comfort, John 14:18. Jesus says, "I will come to you." He is the only Comforter that can get down deep enough to heal wounded hearts. Oh, sorrowing ones, commune with the Comforter that lives in your heart. Listen to him as he makes you remember all the blessed promises of God. That is his office, to bring to your remembrance all that God has told you. John 14:26. In our deep grief we are likely to forget our blessings. God is called a "God of comfort." 2 Cor. 1:3-5. He comforts us through the Holy Spirit, then when comforted, we go and pour out this consolation into other hearts (verse 4).

Our bodies are the temple of the Holy Ghost. God used to manifest his presence in Old Testament times in the tabernacle and the Jewish temple, but in John 4:21-24, Jesus tells the woman of Samaria that he is now going to be worshiped in human hearts. Because God was a spirit, therefore he has sent his Holy Spirit into our hearts so that we can give him real spiritual worship. Now we are his temple. 1 Cor. 3:16-17; 1 Cor. 6:19-20. God has bought our bodies and made them his own. This is the fulfillment of the promise in Isa. 57:15. Now, my beloved, let us keep our bodies pure and clean, for they are the holiest thing on this earth, in fact, the only holy thing on earth. *God's presence in them* makes them holy.

When you believe you are filled with the Spirit as commanded in Eph. 5:18 you will never be drunk, because the spirit of wine and the Spirit of God cannot live together in the same heart. You will also be careful to eat only healthy food and be sure not to eat too much, for the drunkard and glutton are classed together. Prov. 23:21. You will also be careful to keep your bodies clean, your clothes clean, your houses in order, because Jesus lives with you all the time through His Spirit in your bodies. The women who receive the Baptism of the Holy Spirit are careful to keep themselves and their homes clean and in order. The fact that we are indwelt by the Spirit keeps away thoughts of adultery, because the body is the Lord's. 1 Cor. 6:18-20. The Spirit of the Lord is pure and clean.

The Holy Spirit is a person. 1 John 5:6-7, tells us that the Spirit beareth witness; also that the Spirit is truth. Verse 7 puts God, Christ and the Holy Spirit all together as bearing record in heaven. 1 Tim. 4:1 says the Spirit speaketh. It requires a person to speak and to be a witness. Eph. 4:30 tells us not to grieve the Spirit. This proves that the Spirit is a person, the same as God. If he were not a person he could not be grieved nor could he comfort us. I mean the Spirit has feelings. He has life, he can love and be glad, therefore he understands us as a person would. He comes into our life to be a companion with whom we may commune or talk. 2 Cor. 13:14 tells of the "communion of the spirit."

Do not grieve the Spirit. Eph. 4:30 tells us not to grieve the Spirit. We have given our house up to the Holy Spirit, we have asked him to fill every nook and corner of our whole being, body, soul and mind. Remember he is always present. Talk with him. Tell him all our hopes and fears. Be led by him. Rom. 8:14 says: "As many as are led by the Spirit of God they are the sons of God." Do not argue

with the Spirit, but obey him promptly. You know
the fruit of the Spirit mentioned in Gal. 5:22-23. If
your life is full of this fruit the Spirit will be pleased;
if not, he is grieved.

The Holy Spirit reveals Jesus to the Christian.
John 16:14-15. Notice the Spirit conveys to us all
the treasures that Jesus bought for us by his death.
1 Cor. 1:30 tells us Jesus gives us redemption, sanctification, righteousness and wisdom. All these are
given to us through the indwelling Holy Spirit. He
brings us in touch with Jesus, and through him speaks
of himself. The Spirit is modest. John 16:14 says
Jesus is really with us also, and so is the Father.
John 16:15 tells us that all the Father has belongs to
Jesus, therefore, John 14:23 says, the Father, Son and
Holy Spirit all have come to live with us. Praise the
Lord! The Holy Spirit is the medium or channel
through which we receive them. Oh, do not grieve the
Holy Spirit.

Please notice again John 16:13. The Spirit of
Truth guides us into all truth. Jesus is also called
the "Truth." John 14:6. The Spirit guides us to
Christ. He does not speak of himself; the Spirit is
modest. John 16:14, says he will glorify Jesus.
"Christ is all and in all." Col. 3:11 and Col. 2:3-9.
The Spirit gives to us for our daily need these "treasures hidden in Christ." When Jesus was on earth
He gave his Father all the glory. John 17:4; 5:30;
8:29. Thus you see, they glorify each other, and yet
they are all one in this great work of redemption.
Does not this teach us a lesson in humility and mod-
esty? We talk too much about ourselves. Let us

give God all the glory and in "honor prefer one another." Rom. 12:10.

The Holy Spirit has given us the Bible. 2 Pet. 1:20, 21. The Holy Spirit moved the writers of the Bible. He told them what to write. Since the Holy Spirit wrote the Bible, he is the only one that can explain it as it should be. Notice our Bible Band prayer.

O God, help me to remember that thou art talking to me when I read the Bible, and may I believe every word thou sayest. May the Holy Spirit shine in my heart, and make the meaning plain; and make me willing to obey all thy demands. This I ask in Jesus' name, amen.

You need not try to teach the scriptures without the Spirit's power. Read 1 Cor. 2:4 and you will see it was the power of the Holy Spirit that made Paul such a great preacher. Notice Peter's sermon, Acts 2, and Stephen's, Acts 7, and see how much Old Testament they quote. All preachers filled with the Spirit use much of the Bible in their teaching and preaching.

The Holy Spirit uses the Bible. Eph. 6:17 tells us what sword the Spirit uses which is the "word of God." No one need try to work for God till he knows the Bible. D. L. Moody says that he used to pray, asking God to use him. And after awhile he found out there was nothing in him that God could use.

He was not filled with the Holy Spirit, nor did he know his Bible well enough to know what part to read to saint nor what for the sinner, therefore he sought to be filled with the Spirit according to the command in Eph. 5:18, and he got his Bible and began to study it. Soon he was filled with the Spirit, and Bible in hand God used him. Remember, the Bible is one of the tools the Spirit uses.

Jesus used the Bible, when filled with the Spirit. Read Matt. 4:1-11. This was just after Jesus had been anointed with the Holy Spirit, after his baptism. Now he has a battle with Satan and he uses the sword of the Spirit. "It is written" is before every answer he gives to Satan. If you conquer you must quote the Bible when the enemy attacks you. Prayer is good, but will not succeed without the Bible. All the New Testament preachers used the Bible. It is said that Paul's letter to the Romans contains thirty-six quotations from the Old Testament. They believed in the Old Testament. I put this lesson here because I want you more and more to see the value of your Bible study and that the Bible may grow more dear to you every day. Without a knowledge of God's word you will be a poor workman, with it you will be a good one. Read 2 Tim. 2:15. Able to select the right medicine for every human heart you meet. Select it from the Bible, your medicine box.

The Holy Spirit prays for us. Rom. 8:26-27. You have sometimes knelt to pray and you could not utter a word with your lips, but your heart was talking with God. It was the Spirit trying to teach you how to pray. The Spirit was forming your wants into words and telling God what you needed. This is what is meant by "praying in the Spirit." Jude 20, also Eph. 6:18. You are in the Spirit and the Spirit is in you and you do not say your own words, but you wait for the Spirit to tell you what to say when you pray. Then you are sure that you pray according to God's will and you have the answer to your prayer. But if you are not filled with the Spirit then self may come in and ask for what is not God's will.

## Prayer to the Holy Spirit.

"Holy Spirit, light divine,
  Given in our hearts to shine;
  Shed abroad thy brightening rays,
  Help us Jesus' name to praise."
Wisdom from above impart,
Christ enthrone in every heart;
Tune our lips God's praise to sing,
Sanctify our offering.

When to God our hearts would pray,
Teach them, Spirit, what to say;
Make us fully understood
Christ and all he doth command.

Root and ground our souls in love,
Help us all God's will to prove;
With God's fullness fill each heart,
Stay with us and ne'er depart.
            —For "Hope" by Rev. C. P. Jones.

We receive God's love through the Holy Spirit. Rom. 5:1-5 tells us that the child of God can glory in tribulation (verse 3), has patience and hope (verse 4), all because the love of God is shed abroad in his heart. But what brings God's love into his heart? It is "the Holy Ghost which is given unto us." (Verse 5.) Gal. 5:22 tells us that love is the first fruit of the Spirit. But the great thought is that it is God's love that we now have, the kind of love spoken of in John 3:16, a love that will make a great sacrifice to save souls, to save our enemies.

God gave his only son to die for his enemies, not
his friends.  Turn again to Rom. 5:6-9.  Those are
precious words.  They fill my soul with wonder, love
and praise.  Is it possible for us to have such love in
our souls?  Yes.  When the Holy Spirit is shed
abroad in our hearts we really love human souls, and
we would die to save them.  This is one way in which
we can know if we are ''filled with the Spirit.''  The
Spirit fills us with love for those who are lost, a love
like God's love, because this love is born in our hearts
by God's Holy Spirit.  We cannot be successful
Christian workers till we get God's love.  Our love
gives out when those for whom we labor are unjust
and ungrateful.  Oh, I beseech you do not rest till
you are filled with the Holy Spirit.*

The Holy Spirit gives hope.  Did you ever notice
the first page of ''Hope''?  On every copy are these
words: ''Now may the God of hope fill you with all
joy and peace in believing, that ye may abound in
hope through the power of the Holy Ghost.''  Rom.
15:13.  It is a prayer.  It was my prayer for the dear
colored women and children thirteen years ago when
I first began to publish ''Hope.''  They semed so discouraged, and I wanted to encourage them, and that
is why I called my paper ''Hope.''  But I knew the
real hope could only come to them through the Holy
Spirit, therefore I put that prayer in every paper.
If you are ''filled with the Spirit'' you will be hope-

---

*When Hope was first printed, in 1885, our special Bible
verse was Rom. 15:13.  Thirteen years after we added verse
14, because if we obeyed verse 13 we were able ''to admonish
one another.''  Since 1898 to present date, 1912, our verses
are Josh. 1:8, 9.  At first only verse 8, but we could not obey
verse 8 till we believed verse 9.

ful and joyful and peaceful, but it will be God's hope and the "joy of the Lord" and the "peace of God," and you will never be discouraged, no never.

God cannot use those who are discouraged, because discouragement shows lack of faith in our leader and in our cause. A soldier never fights when he believes the enemy will conquer him. Read Josh. 1st chap., and notice how often God exhorts Joshua to "be strong and of good courage." Why? Because God is with him, v. 9. God's presence is the only source of encouragement given us in the whole Bible, because God is sufficient for all things. It is the missionary's outfit.

The Holy Spirit gives us power and this is the greatest of all gifts. Acts 1:8 says, "ye shall receive power, strength." After this power comes upon us and dwells in us "to will and to do," Phil. 2:13, there will be no more whining, "I can't help getting angry, I can't help using beer and tobacco, I can't forgive my neighbor, I can't get time to study my Bible and teach and pray with my children." Why not? because we have *God's power* with us and *can* do all that God commands us. Glory be to his name! This power gives us strength for Christian service. If you have the power to conquer sin and Satan *always,* then you will also be "zealous of good works." All this is proof that you *are* filled with the Holy Spirit. Praise God.

### Book of Acts on the Holy Spirit.

The book of Acts gives us the history of the first Christian church. Surely what these Spirit-filled dis-

ciples said and believed about the work of the Holy
Spirit will be a safeguard for us.

The book of Acts tells us what the disciples did
when filled with the Spirit. Acts 1:2 says through
the Spirit Jesus taught his disciples. Verse 5 of same
chapter He tells them of the Baptism of the Spirit
which was promised in Luke 24:49. Acts 1:8 tells
that *power* would come so that they could *witness.* A
witness tells what he knows of a certain subject or
person. We are to tell what *we know* of *Jesus,* "wit-
neses unto Me." Here is where many of us are weak.
We do not tell what we know about Jesus and His
power to save and comfort. We often talk more
about the devil and bad people than we do about
Jesus. If you have received of Jesus the baptism of
the Holy Spirit be sure you *tell* it in *words,* as well
as in your life, and give all the glory to God and
take none for self.

Our motto is, "Looking Unto Jesus." He is our
pattern. Jesus was anointed with the Holy Spirit
in answer to prayer. Luke 3:21-22. He was full of
the Spirit. Luke 4:1. And was "led by the Spirit"
and conquered Satan through the Spirit." "Returned
in the power of the Spirit" to Galilee. Luke 4:14.
The Spirit was upon Him as He taught the Bible,
Luke 4:18-19. There is only *one* Holy Spirit. We,
too, are sons of God, John 1:12, and may *expect* the
*same Spirit* to help us in all we do, in the hour of
temptation as well as when we teach the Bible. Acts
10:38 tells us what the Spirit did for Jesus in his
human nature. He will do the same for us. Then
*we* shall "go about doing good." Doing good is
not carrying idle tales from door to door.

## Jesus Is My Friend.

"I've found a friend in Jesus,—He's everything to me;
  He's the fairest of ten thousand to my soul!
The 'Lily of the Valley,' in Him alone I see
  All I need to cleanse and make me fully whole:
In sorrow He's my comfort, in trouble He's my stay;
  He tells me every care on Him to roll;
He's the 'Lily of the Valley,' the Bright and Morning Star;
  He's the fairest of ten thousand to my soul!"
In sorrow He's my comfort, in trouble He's my stay;
  He tells me every care on Him to roll:
He's the "Lily of the Valley," the Bright and Morning Star;
  He's the fairest of ten thousand to my soul!

He all my grief has taken, and all my sorrows borne;
  In temptation He's my strong and mighty tower;
I've all for Him forsaken, I've all my idols torn
  From my heart, and now He keeps me by His power.
Though all the world forsake me, and Satan tempts me sore,
  Through Jesus I shall safely reach the goal;
He's the "Lily of the Valley," the Bright and Morning Star;
  He's the fairest of ten thousand to my soul!

He'll never, never leave me, nor yet forsake me here,
  While I live by faith, and do His blessed will;
A wall of fire about me, I've nothing now to fear
  With His manna He my hungry soul shall fill.
When crowned at last in glory, I'll see His blessed face,
  Where rivers of delight shall ever roll;
He's the "Lily of the Valley," the Bright and Morning Star;
  He's the fairest of ten thousand to my soul!"
                                        —*Gospel Hymns.*

Acts 1:9-11 and Rom. 8:34 tell us Jesus had gone
back to His seat at God's right hand. The disciples
into the upper room in Jerusalem to *pray.* Remember
they *prayed.* Acts 1:15 says there were not only

twelve, but in all one hundred and twenty present.
Here they waited till Acts 2:1-4, when they received
the answer to their prayer. Verses 16-18 tell us this
was promised long before it occurred. On the *women*
as well as the *men* came the Holy Ghost. Acts 2:17-
18. It would pay those of us who do not have this
wonderful power of the Spirit to wait in prayer and
humble confession till we receive Him. Do we believe
that *this* is for *us* as well as the command for water
baptism, about which so much has been spoken and
written? You remember John said we should *expect*
this baptism. John 1:32-33, Matt. 3:11. Strange,
is it not, that we have caught at the shadow and for-
gotten the substance? The water baptism is only
a picture of the higher baptism of the Holy Spirit,
which comes to us when we are crucified with Christ.
Rom. 6:3-7. Can you truly say:

> "I am crucified with Jesus,
>    And He lives and dwells in me;
> I have ceased from all my struggling,
>    'Tis no longer I but He;
>   All my will is yielded to Him,
>    And His Spirit reigns within,
>   And His precious blood each moment
>    Keeps me cleansed and free from sin."
>                          —*Rev. A. B. Simpson.*

Let us look at Acts 2:32-33, which is a part of
Peter's sermon, where he witnesses to Christ's resur-
rection and tells that Jesus is *now* exalted, placed on
high with God. Notice the words "Having received
of the Father the *promise* of the Holy Ghost which
was shed forth." God had *promised* this gift, the
wonderful gift of the Holy Spirit, but it was given

in *answer to Jesus' prayer*, John 14:16, "I will pray the Father." Jesus' work for us now is prayer. Heb. 7:25. His first great prayer was for the Holy Spirit, and the *Spirit came.* Stop and *think* and *pray* and *thank God* right here. God knew what His children needed and He promised the Spirit, but since Christ is our redeemer *all* blessings come to us *through Him.* So it was necessary that He should depart and take his place as our intercessor before the Spirit could come. John 16:5-7. Verse 7, "It is expedient," or necessary, that Jesus go away. How we should value this great gift. With Him comes *power* and all things we need.

Acts 2:38, 39. Peter tells them to repent and be baptized and receive the gift of the Holy Spirit." He is a *gift.* All we can do is to *give up all* and we shall receive Him. It means an entire surrender of *self.* If in your hands you hold a waiter full of dishes while I hand you this paper, before you can take it you must put down the waiter; if your heart and hands are full of self and worldly pleasure then you must make an entire surrender of yourself to God, and He will empty you and fill you with His Spirit. I do not know that the whole 3,000 that were added to the church that day received this gift. The record does not say that they did. It was their privilege the same as yours and mine; but you know that *all* have not received this blessing who are *now* added to the church. The Holy Spirit is given in answer to prayer. Acts 4:23-31 tells of a prayer meeting that brought another Pentecost like the one in Acts, and they got the answer to their prayer, which was that they might "speak the word of God with boldness." We all need the *power* of the Holy Spirit in order to teach God's word on the subject of Holy living. Many think they can be Christians and live in sin every day. This is wrong. 1 Peter 1:13-16.

Acts 5:1-11. You notice in Acts 4:34-37 that many of those who were converted sold their lands, or at least a part of them, and gave the price to the disciples, so that they might be able to help all among them that needed help. I wish we had a plan like this in our churches today. Then no one would suffer need. But the sad story of Ananias and wife shows that they tried to deceive whom? Peter? No, but the Holy Spirit. Verse 3. The Holy Spirit is a person. He had charge of the church. He has charge of it today. He guides you and me to *give* if we give *to Him*, but when we give for show, as we often do at these rallies for money and to get our names in print, then Satan has deceived *us* and made us do wrong as he did Ananias. You can see, Ananias wanted to have the *name* of giving *all he had*. He might have given a *part* and said, "It is only a *part* of the price of the land I sold." But no, he was like these people who give to have their name published or praised. Remember, you cannot deceive the Holy Spirit. He knows the *motive* for which you give, and He is grieved when you give for show. For such a gift you *have* your pay and will get *no* reward in heaven. Matthew 6:1-4. It is *very* wicked in our pastors to thus tempt their people to give for show, as they do at these rallies. Why do they not teach them to quietly, *at home*, on their knees, lay aside what they *can* donate and modestly hand it in, not letting "their right hand know what their left hand does?" Then would they get their reward in heaven. Matthew 6:3-4.

Acts 6:1-5. The money that was put into the hands of the disciples, to give to the poor, needed so much attention as the church grew larger that they must have help. You see by verse 1 that it was given out *daily*. The disciples called the whole church together and said: "Here is a work to do that is not exactly teaching the Bible, as we do, but it is just as important. No one can do it except filled with the Holy Ghost." You see how much this New Testament church depended on the Holy Spirit. How have we lost sight of this great gift. I say lost sight, because he is so seldom spoken of in connection with service. These were not deacons; if so, the deacons of today do not *daily* hunt up the poor and supply their needs out of a fund that the church has in charge. These men also taught and preached as they had opportunity. Indeed, I suppose the whole church in those days were workers and teachers, as the Spirit led them. Different gifts, but the *same Spirit*. 1 Cor. 12:4-12. I wish we all had our special line of work to do today and would do it in the *power* of *the Spirit*.

## What Are the Tools That the Holy Spirit Uses?

The answer to this question will help us in our study of the subject.

Ephesians 6:17-19. Here we have two of the tools that the Holy Spirit uses in His work. As I write this lesson I need both; as you read it you need the same. First the word of God—the Bible—which is the "Sword of the Spirit." These words that we read with our eyes are cold and lifeless till the Holy Spirit takes them and puts fire and life into them. We must expect the Spirit to open these Scriptures to us as Jesus did to the disciples. Luke 24:32. Second tool is prayer. The prayer is *in the Spirit.* The *Spirit tells us how to pray,* or prays *in us,* and gives us power to persevere in prayer. With Paul, in verse 19, I beg you to "pray for me," and may it be a prayer in the Spirit, and when you have studied this lesson may the same Spirit open your mouth, dear reader, while you read and teach it to your neighbors. We have the "word" and "prayer," but both are worthless except as they are used by the Spirit. You see, beloved Bible readers, how much we need the baptism of the Holy Spirit, so that we may profitably study the Bible, also pray an acceptable prayer.

## The Bible and the Holy Spirit.

I see! I see! just what I need.
It is that I should stop and read—
Read the Word that gives me light,
Seek the Spirit that gives me might.

It is the Word and Spirit, too,
That I would recommend to you;
For God hath given both to me,
And they have made me glad and free.
            —*For Hope, by Rev. W. H. Smith.*

We want you to notice a sermon preached by a man who used the sword of the Spirit. Acts 7th chapter gives you the sermon. Acts 6:5 says he was full of faith and the Holy Ghost; verse 8 says he was full of faith and *power*. You remember the Holy Ghost gives *power*, gives courage, gives joy, gives wisdom, gives all we need for service. Notice verse 15. He had a shining, happy face. He had the *Spirit, one* of the tools that God uses; then chapter 7 of Acts shows us that he also had the other tool, the "word of God." His sermon was nearly all quotations from the Old Testament, the only Scriptures they had in those days. I wish I could make you see how important it is to be full of the Bible. This book of the law should never depart out of your mouth, Josh. 1:8. There was a man once who used to often pray "Lord, use me in your work." A friend showed him that he did not know the Bible, neither was he full of the Spirit, and those two things were *all God could use.*

Acts 7:51. Stephen told these Jews that they *resisted* the Holy Spirit. The Holy Spirit speaks to all hearts. Some hearts *open* and take Him in and are *saved;* others *resist* and are *lost,* v. 52. The "Just one" means Jesus. Have you counted the number of names given to the Savior? V. 55 tells us again that he was full of the Spirit. This death of Stephen is so sweet, so comforting. It thrills my very soul. What did Stephen care for the stones, while gazing into heaven he saw his blessed Saviour standing ready to receive his faithful servant? This death is the most wonderful of any recorded in the Bible, except that of the Lord Jesus. In many things they are alike because they have the same Holy Spirit working in them to will and to do. Jesus prayed for His mur-

derers. Luke 23:24. Stephen did the same. Acts
7:60. Stephen "fell asleep," he did not die, 1 Thess.
4:14, "asleep *in Jesus*," blessed sleep. Let us prayerfully bow before God and ask the Holy Spirit to teach
us this lesson.

Persecution never stops the work of the Lord. Going
*with* the *world* is what weakens the church, but resist-
ing sin of all kinds gives us power to do *more* work
and convict sinners, because this shows that our re-
ligion means more to us than *our life.*

## "Fear Not, I Am with Thee."

How firm a foundation, ye saints of the Lord,
Is laid for your faith in his excellent word:
What more can he say than to you he hath said,
To you, who for refuge to Jesus have fled.
Fear not, I am with thee; Oh, be not dismayed,
For I am thy God, and will still give thee aid:
I'll strengthen thee, help thee, and cause thee to stand,
Upheld by my righteous, omnipotent hand.

When through deep waters I call thee to go,
The rivers of sorrow shall not overflow;
For I will be with thee thy trials to bless,
And sanctify to thee thy deepest distress.

The soul that on Jesus hath leaned for repose,
I will not, I will not desert to his foes:
That soul, though all hell should endeavor to shake,
I'll never—no, never—no, never forsake.
                          —*Rippon Selection,* 1718.

Acts 8:1-17. A great revival in Samaria, where
Jesus preached two days, John 4:40. They believed
and were baptized with water. Did Peter and John
(v. 14-17) set these young converts at collecting money

to build a new church edifice, or at any other work? No, verily. But they told them of that higher Christian life that comes to us through the *gift* of the Holy Ghost. O God, give to our young converts in the city of Nashville this blessed gift of the Holy Spirit, so that they may be able to overcome the world, the flesh and the devil. The Spirit gives full assurance and takes all doubts away. 1 John 4:13. Have *you* the Holy Spirit in its fullness? If so, you are ready to give money and do work for God, of *all* kinds, with the *right motive*.

Acts 8:29-40. The Holy Spirit was with Philip. He was one of the seven chosen. The Spirit guides. John 16:13. Guides in the *little* things; made Philip go up to that stranger in his chariot and ask him what might be thought a rude question. But the Spirit opened the way and the Spirit taught him how to explain Isa. 53:6-8, and the same Spirit opened the heart of the Eunuch to receive the message. It is easy working when filled with the Spirit. Notice verse 39. The same Spirit took Philip away to another point, Azotus, where he had other work to do. The Spirit *is our guide*. We should depend more on Him and less on our own judgment, and yet we must be sure that it is the Holy Spirit and not a temptation of the devil. If we are very careful not to *grieve* the Spirit by wrong doing, Eph. 4:30-31, then we will all *know His voice*. Sin dulls our spiritual ears.

Let us study Paul's first prayer. Acts 9:6. "Lord, what wilt thou have me do?" shows that Paul had then submitted his *will* to Christ, and yet he had not been baptized with water or the Holy Spirit. We know what Paul did those three days in which his natural eyes were blind, v. 11. We know also that he saw a vision telling him what to do, v. 12. This shows that Paul was in communion with God, was converted before Ananias came to him, v. 17. Ananias calls him *"Brother Saul*, I have come to tell you about the baptism of the Holy Spirit and to baptize you with water." V. 20 says he "straightway preached Christ," v. 22 and *"increased* in strength." Paul has much to say about the Holy Spirit in his writings. We should study this beginning of his ministry. He was *obedient*. He *taught about Jesus*. He *grew* in *grace*. 2 Pet. 3:17-18.

Turn to Acts 10. This is a very important chapter. It should be memorized. Preaching the gospel to the Gentiles. Begun by Peter, but to Paul was this work specially given. Gal. 2:7-8. To open this door to the Gentiles required first a vision, Acts 10:11-15, then the Holy Spirit spoke to Peter (verses 19-20), telling him *to go* and doubt not. A vision in answer to prayer had prepared Cornelius and his friends to receive the good news. Then Peter's sermon (verses 34-43), followed by the baptism of the Holy Spirit, even before the water baptism. This was necessary to *convince* Peter that God really called the Gentiles to the same privileges that the Jews enjoyed. Commit verse 43. Praise God! Salvation and remission of sins is *free* for *all* the human family. Oh, let us hasten and carry it to the "isles of the sea," to the ends of the earth.

Acts 13:1-12. In Acts 13:1-7, the church is being taught by the Holy Spirit to do aggressive mission

work.  Too many workers in the home church and no
one telling the poor heathen of Jesus' love and power
to save.  This came in answer to *fasting* and *prayer*.
Do you think we fast and pray as much these days
as we should?  The evil spirit of selfishness and covet-
ousness now in our churches would be *cast out* if we
had more prayer and fasting.  Matt. 17:19-21.  You
remember Acts 1:8 told us that when we receive the
*power* of the Holy Spirit that we would be *witnesses* of Jesus and his love, not only in Judea and
Samaria, but to the "uttermost parts of the earth,"
which means all the heathen world.  You know that
there are nearly 856,000,000 of human beings who
have never yet heard the name of Jesus.  Oh, how our
careless selfishness must grieve the Holy Spirit, which
Spirit is constantly saying, "Separate us to the work
whereunto we are called," Acts 13:2, the work of
missions.  Have you ever noticed the way in which
all our money and time is used to keep *our own home
church up,* whereas every church of one hundred
members ought to be able to support one missionary
to the heathen.  What is in the way?  Answer:  The
*members are not filled with the Holy Spirit.*

## Speed Away with the Gospel.

"Speed away, speed away on your mission of light,
To the lands that are lying in darkness and night;
'Tis the Master's command; go ye forth in his name,
The wonderful gospel of Jesus proclaim;
Take your lives in your hand, to the work while 'tis day,
Speed away, speed away, speed away."
Speed away, speed away with the life-giving Word,
To the nations that know not the voice of the Lord;
Take the wings of the morning and fly o'er the wave,
In the strength of your Master the lost ones to save;
He is calling once more, not a moment's delay,
Speed away, speed away, speed away.

Speed away, speed away with the message of rest,
To the souls by the tempter in bondage oppressed;
For the Saviour has purchased their ransom from sin,
And the banquet is ready, oh, gather them in;
To the rescue make haste, there's no time for delay,
Speed away, speed away, speed away."

*—Gospel Hymns.*

Chapter 13 of Acts also shows how God is opening the way for Paul to teach the Gentiles. (Verses 44-52.) Memorize verses 46-47. "Salvation to the ends of the earth." Praise God! Verse 52. "Filled with joy and the Holy Ghost." The Comforter was *always* with those early missionaries and kept them full of joy and hope in the midst of persecutions and trials of all kinds. I want you long-faced, gloomy Christians to notice this fact. God wants his children joyful. John 15:11. "My joy." Jesus' joy is always fresh and overflowing. O God, fill us anew *today* with the Holy Spirit!

Turn to Acts 15:6-11. Notice verse 8. The great

proof that the Gentiles were called the same as the Jews was that they *received the gift of the Holy Ghost.* It is through the indwelling of this same Spirit in *all* hearts of *all* nations that makes us all "one in Christ Jesus." Unless we have the *mind* of Christ we are not his children. We get Christ's mind and character *through the Holy Spirit,* which we accept by faith (verse 9) and then our hearts are purified (verse 11). All nations saved alike. The gift of the Holy Spirit puts us in communion with Christ and through Him with God. "Let us meditate on these things." 1 Tim. 4:14-16. Oh, for more thought and quiet meditation and prayer and a willingness to be "*led* by the Spirit." Then shall we be able "to save ourselves and them that hear us," v. 16.

Read Acts 15:23-29. This is the first "circular letter" sent to all the churches after the meeting of this *first* council. Notice the kind way in which they refer to their *first* mission arises, Paul and Barnabas (vs. 25-26). Notice also v. 28. The Holy Spirit *presided at this meeting.* They knew the Holy Spirit was pleased with their decision. Do you not think it would be a good plan to often stop business in our associations and conventions and ask the Holy Spirit what *He thinks,* and get *quiet* before Him so that we can *hear His* voice? There is too much noise and not enough Bible and prayer mixed with all our business. We forget that it is not *our* work but *God's* work that we are doing, and therefore God should be consulted every step of the way. God is the *presiding* officer, but on we go, without even *recognizing His presence.*

What shameful disrespect! Let us pray for the leaders of our religious gatherings. The Holy Spirit is greatly grieved by the disorder, envy, jealousy and self-seeking so often manifested in these meetings.

The Holy Ghost forbade these missionaries to go to Asia. Acts 16:6-10. By this we know that these missionaries took the Spirit as *their guide*. They were in such close communion that they knew His voice. Next they tried to go to Bithynia, v. 7, but the Spirit stopped them. In v. 9 they got the clear guidance. God wanted the gospel preached in Europe. As you read on through the chapter you see that doors opened, but sometimes opened through great suffering. That prison in Philippi was the greatest pulpit Paul could have had. Prayer and praise shook the walls, converted the jailer and spread the news far and near as it could not have been done had no persecution come to them. It is always safe to follow the teachings of the Spirit, though it may lead to great suffering. While doing work for God we are often discouraged because success does not crown our efforts *immediately*. We have great need of patience. Heb. 10:36. The Captain of our salvation was made perfect through suffering. Heb. 2:10. "The servant is not above his master."

Read Acts 19:1-7. It seems as if the first question that Paul asked those who professed to be Christians was, "Have you received the Holy Ghost since you believed?" This question ought to be asked oftener than it is. Each individual should ask *himself* the question and not rest till he got a decided answer. We know that these disciples did not hear *all* that John taught. They seemed simply to have heard of the *water* baptism, and that is the way with the most of us today. You remember, Matt. 3:11, that John told them of the baptism of the *Holy Ghost*, but since there may have been no *written* word for the teachers to read, it is no wonder that mistakes were made. But with the New Testament in our hands today *we need* make no mistake. They received the Spirit, v. 6.

Notice Acts 20:22-24. Paul expected persecutions. The Holy Spirit *taught* him that truth. Paul was not "carried to heaven on 'flowery beds of ease'" nor will any other true follower. It is the truly godly Christians that suffer these God sent persecutions. 2 Tim. 3:12. Commit Acts 20:24, and let none of my readers be moved and troubled because of a little suffering for the cause of Christ. Be brave, be courageous, and *finish* the work God has given you to do, and, like Paul, you will get the crown. 2 Tim. 4:7, 8. I find so many of our Fireside Pupils and Bible Band workers who give up because every one does not appreciate their work. Shame, shame on such poor soldiers! Notice the blessed result of suffering for Christ's sake. 2 Cor. 4:17, 18.

Beloved friends, we have certainly learned that there *is a Holy Ghost;* that he taught and guided the early Christian Church, whose history we find in the book of Acts. The great question for each of us to settle is this: "Am I *filled* with this same Spirit?" Not simply to know I have been converted. We know that it was by the Spirit that we were convicted of sin and led to Christ, John 16:8, but have you, since your conversion, surrendered your whole being to God and let Him *fill* you with Himself through the Holy Spirit? Are you *all* the Lord's? You *are* the Temple of God, 1 Cor. 3:16, but does *He fill* His temple or does He only occupy one room in His temple? These are the questions that must be settled if we expect to be a success as a Christian.

How can I know that I am filled with the Holy Spirit? you ask. I answer, in the same way that you know a tree, by its fruit. Have we the "fruit of the Spirit," as found in Gal. 5:22-25? This is the "Search light" and will reveal to us our true situation. We each one *know* if we are meek and gentle and *filled* with love and joy and peace. We know it by v. 25. "Walk," here means our *every day conduct*. We say we live in the Spirit, or have the Spirit's *life in our souls,* if so, it will lead us to *walk right.* It is one thing to *say* "I am filled with the Spirit," but quite a different thing to have a *daily* "walk" that *proves* it. I am sure we all *long* to live a higher and better life than we live today, but have we that mighty power of the Spirit in our souls that gives us constant victory over sin? If not, what is the reason? Study patiently and prayerfully what the Bible tells us about God the Father, God the Son, and God the Holy Spirit.

We will look again at John 16:5-24. When the Spirit came he was to guide us into all truth. Verse 13. "He will not speak of Himself." Verse 14. He will "glorify Jesus and will receive of *Jesus* the things we need and show them to us." Verse 15. Jesus' things mean *all* that the Father has, therefore through the

Spirit we get all the treasures of heaven, but we really get Jesus. John 14:23. Jesus is still with us through His Spirit. Life, *our* life, is *in Christ*, and Christ comes and lives His life in us through the Spirit. This is the way we get the "mind of Christ." 1 Cor. 2:16. Is not this a wonderful assertion, to say, "*We have the mind of Christ?*" It all comes through the indwelling of the Spirit. Dear reader, have *you* the Holy Spirit? Does He fill your soul and take posession of your whole life, so that you always do the things that please Him because you are led by Him? Rom. 8:14.

Jesus came to show us the Father. Through him God was manifest or seen in human form. 1 Tim. 3:16. "Jesus is the image of the invisible God." Col. 1:15. The Holy Spirit now shows us the Christ and the Father also. We must not separate the Holy Spirit and Christ. John 16:14 tells us the Holy Spirit brings to us the things of Christ. He lives in us; yes, fills our heart and brings us Christ, who is our *light* and *life*. Col. 3:4. When Jesus left earth He said to His disciples, "Lo, *I* am with you always," and so He is through *His* Spirit. There is only *one* Holy Spirit and His presence gives us God the Father and God the Son. John 14:23. God is a Spirit. John 4:24. We cannot understand all this, but we believe that we have the presence of the God-head with us always, through the *one Holy Spirit*. We believe it because God says so. Oh, how glorious to have the fellowship of *heaven* in our daily life on *earth*. This is heaven on earth.

## "Jesus Gave Himself for Me."

"Once it was the blessing, now it is the Lord;
Once it was the feeling, now it is His Word.
Once His gifts I wanted, now Himself alone;
Once I sought for healing, now the Healer own."

CHORUS.

All in all, forever, Jesus will I sing,
Everything in Jesus, and Christ in everything.

Once 'twas painful trying, now 'tis perfect trust;
Once a half salvation, now the uttermost;
Once 'twas ceaseless holding, now he holds me fast;
Once 'twas constant drifting, now my anchor's cast.

Once 'twas busy planning, now 'tis trustful prayer;
Once 'twas anxious caring, now he has the care;
Once 'twas what I wanted, now what Jesus says;
Once 'twas constant asking, now 'tis ceaseless praise.

Once it was my working, His it hence shall be;
Once I tried to use him, now he uses me.
Once the power I wanted, now the Mighty One;
Once I worked for glory, now his will alone.

Once I hoped in Jesus, now I know He's mine;
Once my lamps were dying, now they brightly shine;
Once for death I waited, now his coming hail,
And my hopes are anchored safe within the veil."
—*By Rev. A. B. Simpson.*

Many times have we listened to the minister pronouncing the benediction or blessing found in 2 Cor. 13:14, but have we ever looked closely into it? First is the grace or loving favor of Jesus who died to save us from our sins. Next love, the never failing love of God the Father. Then communion of the Holy

Spirit. Communion means intercourse, fellowship, conversation. He is the medium through which we talk with God. This is the reason that a sin against the Holy Spirit is the worst of all sins. Such a sin shuts us off from God. Let us be careful not to grieve the Holy Spirit. Eph. 4:30. He is the proof of our salvation. Through Him we call God Father. His Spirit tells us we are His children. Rom. 8:15-16. May the Holy Spirit enlighten your understanding as you read.

As I write these lines I feel more and more how weak I am. All my lessons are worthless except through the power of the Holy Spirit, therefore we bow together and pray this prayer, Heb. 13:20-21, "The God of peace through the blood or redemption of Christ, make us *perfect* in *every good* work, *working in us* that which in his sight is well pleasing through Christ. Amen!" It is the living, resurrected Christ living His *life in us* through the Spirit that does the work. We simply *give up all* and let Him into *His* temple, which is the human heart, and He cleans it out and takes full possession, just as far as we will *let* him rule in us and work in us. Remember, sin grieves the Spirit. Let *God keep you* from sinning. Christ came to destroy the work of the devil and *He is able to keep* you from falling. Heb. 7:25. Praise his name!

But after all these Bible lessons and explanations of the same, yet I hear a tired, discouraged voice saying, "It is all very beautiful and comforting, but *how* am I to get this power of the Holy Spirit that gives me the victory over sin? Oh, I am tired

of sin. I want to overcome. I want to conquer
Satan." My beloved friend, I can only say over and
over again, "Believe in the Lord Jesus and thou shalt
be saved from sin." "A Savior *from* sin," is Jesus'
name. Matt. 1:21. As ye have received Christ by
faith you must walk the Christian life by the same
*faith.* Col. 2:6-7. The just (the justified ones) shall
*live* by faith. Heb. 10:38-39. We receive the filling
of the Holy Spirit by *faith* just the same as we
received forgiveness of sins. The different gifts of
the Spirit come to us in the same way. 1 Cor. 12:
4-12. The power of the Spirit that gives us victory
over sin of any kind comes to us by faith. For
example, I am tempted to be proud. I have no
strength to resist, but I submit myself to God. James
4:7. I turn the tempter over to the Holy Spirit who
is always with me. I say, "Drive away this devil;
I have no power, but you have all power." Then I
*believe,* and in a minute I am as humble as a child.
Again the Spirit is with me for service. I have break-
fast to get; it must be ready by 6 a. m. I believe I
have faith that God will wake me in time, and that
the Holy Spirit will make me remember to get things
ready as far as possible the night before. I trust
him for strength for this service, and I get it and
praise the Lord because my *every* day work is as
much a service for the Lord as teaching a sinner the
way to Christ. A mother prays that her children
may be able and willing to help her in the work of
the house. She trusts that the Holy Spirit will work
in them to do it and make her wise and patient in
showing them how to help. She has *faith* and the

work is done. This is the way that we *live* a *life* of
victory and sing a song of praise all day long. The
mother might *pray* and not *believe* and her children
would be as wayward as ever. Her *faith* makes her
watchful and dependent on the Holy Spirit's power.
Prayer without faith is of no use. Why not believe
God when he says "I am a very present help in
trouble." Ps. 46:1. You believe your children, your
neighbor, though they sometimes tell lies. Why not
believe "God who cannot lie?" I almost forgot to
say that you must *obey* as well as trust. Acts 5:32
says that God gives the Holy Spirit to those who
obey. When you read a command in the Bible say
immediately, "O God, I will do as you say," and
*do it*. God will give you the power to obey. Is it
plain now? Do you see the way to this life, this
abundant life in Christ? If so, praise the Lord!

## "Christ Is All."

### GAL. 3:11.

"I ENTERED once a home of care,
 For age and penury were there,
  Yet peace and joy withal;
 I asked the lonely mother whence
 Her helpless widowhood's defense,
  She told me 'Christ was all.'"

CHORUS.

||: Christ is all, all in all,
 Yes, Christ is all in all. :||

I stood beside a dying bed,
Where lay a child with aching head,
  Waiting for Jesus' call;
I marked his smile, 'twas sweet as May,
And as his spirit passed away,
  He whispered, "Christ is all."
I saw the gospel herald go,—
To Afric's sand and Greenland's snow,
  To save from Satan's thrall;
Nor home nor life he counted dear,
'Midst wants and perils owned no fear,
  He felt that "Christ is all."

Then come to Christ, oh, come to-day,
The Father, Son, and Spirit say.
  The Bride repeats the call;
For He will cleanse your guilty stains,
His love will soothe your weary pains,
  For "Christ is all in all."
                    —From "Cheerful Songs."

## Power and Gladness Through the Holy Spirit.

Written for HOPE by Rev. C. P. Jones.
Tune—"He is Just the Same Today."
Ye shall receive power after that the Holy Ghost is come upon you.—Acts 1:8.
Have you learned the precious secret of the Holy Spirit's power?
Do you know that joy and gladness is your portion every hour?
Do you know that you may always have the Spirit dwell within?
And that Jesus Christ within you sanctifies and keeps from sin?

### Chorus.

Oh, be filled, be filled, my brother, with the Holy Spirit's power,
Only ask, and God will send him like an overflowing shower.
  Oh, be filled with Holy Spirit's power.
Oh, my brother, Jesus never meant for you and me to stay
In the flesh, and feebly struggle to obey Him day by day.

In the flesh we cannot please Him, nor the works of heaven do;
Jesus Christ has something better than this struggling life for
you.

He has sent the Holy Spirit to fulfill in us the right;
We surrender and receive Him, then He strengthens us with
might.
And the deeds of grace we're doing and the life we thenceforth
live
Is no longer ours; but Jesus through our faith His life doth
give.

Do you find it hard, my brother, to obey the law of love?
Is your heart so cold toward Jesus that your faith you cannot
prove?
Oh, my brother, claim the Spirit, for the promise is to you,
And the Spirit needs you, brother, for laborers are few.

## We Want Sunshiny Christians.

"Light is sown for the righteous, and gladness for the upright in heart."—Ps. 97:11.

"Rejoice in the Lord always, and again I say rejoice,"—Phil. 4:4.

"Arise and shine for thy light has come and the glory of the Lord is risen upon thee."—Is. 60:1.

But be sure to shine *so* "that you may *glorify your Father in Heaven.*"—Matt. 5:16.

"God is light and in him is no darkness."—1 John 1:5-7.

"I am the light of the world. He that *followeth* me shall not walk in darkness but shall have the light of life."—John 8:12.

The whole world was lost in the darkness of sin,
    The Light of the world is Jesus;
Like sunshine at noonday His glory shone in,
    The Light of the world is Jesus.

    Come to the Light, 'tis shining for thee;
    Sweetly the Light has dawned upon me.
    Once I was blind but now I can see;
        The Light of the world is Jesus.

No darkness have we who in Jesus abide,
    The Light of the world is Jesus;
We walk in the Light when we follow our Guide,
    The Light of the world is Jesus.

*—Gospel Hymns.*